OSTRACA

T0096023

Poetry by Gabriel Levin

SLEEPERS OF BEULAH
(1992)

GABRIEL LEVIN

Ostraca

ANVIL PRESS POETRY

ACKNOWLEDGEMENTS

Some of the poems in this collection originally appeared
in *Agenda, Arc, London Magazine, Metre, Modern Poetry in Translation,
The Jewish Quarterly, The Turret Bookstore Broadside, Verse.*

Published in Great Britain in 1999
by Anvil Press Poetry
Neptune House 70 Royal Hill London SE10 8RF

ISBN 0 85646 317 5

Copyright © Gabriel Levin 1999

This book is published
with financial assistance from
The Arts Council of England

Set in Monotype Janson by Anvil
Printed in Great Britain
by The Cromwell Press Trowbridge Wilts

A catalogue record for this book
is available from The British Library

The moral rights of the author
have been asserted in accordance with
the Copyright, Designs and Patents Act, 1988

for Noa

Contents

Ostraca

IMAGO

After a dozen molts at least
like so many drafts lobbed
into the bin, you reach the point

of no return, and squat
immobile and dumb, in brackish
waters, captive to a blank

reverie, as your long lip
is sucked in and the crumpled wads
in your wing pads twitch. Un-

lovely nymph, what dim larval
urge prods you up the stem
to light and air? The cuticle

that sheathed the tacit self
splits open, and you emerge,
jewel-eyed, instantly on the wing.

INLAY

In soft ivory Ashtoreth-at-the-Window
    stares at me with her one good eye.
    For three days now she's fixed
        her blunt gaze,
made more penetrating by the tiny hole
    drilled in the pupil,
on my own figure washed in shadows
    and indeterminate.

No matter how I fidget in my chair
    or wander, boy-errant, in my mind
    she's there, nooked above
        my left shoulder, leaning on the balustrade
and giving me that absorbed
    look, dissembling
interest, as if I were the lure
    in the stolid air.

QUARRY

              . . . Then we piled
into the old Mercedes, diesel-fueled
    and lumbersome, nosing out of the city,
past the first roadblock, picking up speed,
    bearing us further into the territories
where men debouch at dawn
    and re-enter at dusk, coated in lime dust.
Nablus trussed against the flanks
    of the mountain, like quarry; or so the city
recomposes itself in memory,
    its grey wash of stone and concrete
hardening into a grimace
    of its former self.
               "Exquisite
Nablous, what a Paradise
    to rest in," Elizabeth Butler
writes to her mother, Sunday, 19th
    of April 189–, after eight
hours in the saddle. Orange and pomegranate
    trees, a Syrian fumbling at the keys
of the harmonium in the presbytery—
    such sweet reveries in Neapolis:

"A Turkish sentry came and lit his fire
    close to our tents, and was suffered
to mount his quite unnecessary guard
    over us all night, with an eye
to baksheesh at sunrise."
                 Plump pastoral.
    Now as then, *spoil speedeth,*
prey hasteth, written in a large,

legible hand across the open
highlands, the blessing and the curse;
   the hair-pin turns
down to the great plain;
   someone muttering
into his beard: "See, there come people
   down by the middle ('navel')
of the land." Or words to that effect—
   ghosting what distant vision?

* * *

Beautiful mountain, what latecoming
   clouds your summit, and who goes there
in the shade of your pine grove? The good
   Samaritans peer out of their windows:
look how the young parade
   their curiosity.
               —Lofty country,
a host of well-wishers trudges
   up your slumbering mound of ruins.

Jebel Tor, who measured your girth
   and counted the steps of your stairway?
Who minted your coins, lovely Luzah,
   and plumbed your quarry?
So we stood at last, short of breath,
   on Mt Gerizim, seeming even to ourselves
humbled like the shade-seeking birds
   in the trees: open-beaked, wings
slightly raised, releasing the day's heat.

SAHARA

The sand grouse, vigilant and swift—
not its black, bungling

European counterpart, with lyre-

shaped tail and disyllabic
sneezing note—leaves its sleeping

hollow in the stony wastes,
whirrs down by the fossil

rain, cupped in weathered rock,

and nimbly fills its crop for the day
with dregs of the deluge.

OSTRACON I

Blunt as a hardwood door
and sleek in oil, I see them
ready for battle.
Tell them how it was, the rooting out
and pulling down.
              Slingers in spike hats, and bowmen,
storm-troopers ducking behind
the engines of wrath, as a fallout
of debris and flaming brands
blights the air around the gate tower.

Tell them how it was, thrashing for words
like a bagged fowl in the guardhouse
"This very day, this very day . . . "

MEDUSA

R.F.

That morning we spotted a dozen, or more:
some, recently disgorged, resembled
a child's smudged, see-through umbrella,
as the slow sweeping tide nudged their bodies—
exposed and gelatinous—while others,
half-buried, seemed no more than patties,
the fat, tentacled mouth, gleaming in the sun.
We edged forward cautiously,
and circled the beached swimming-bell,
knowing full well how bathers,
unknowingly grazing the limpid disc,
were left smarting for hours,
though now we applauded whenever the surf
rolled further up the shore and briefly
glossed with foam what seemed inert,
and clapped again if it slapped and buoyed
and dragged the sluggish sac back into
the sea. "I remained," the old poet's words
surged from within, as the children ran ahead,
"like a medusa on the shore."

And though the *Ethics of the Fathers* speak
of vestibule and banquet hall, I prefer
your plainspoken, "room upon room,"
in the great metaphysical house by the sea,
where you wandered, dazed,
as a young man—room upon unearthly room,
in which the venturing mind glanced off the objects
of its quest, and recoiled; for you were quick
to realize, even as you thought to taste such strange,

unrealizable fruit, that the dream had no core.
So you tossed and woke uncomforted,
restless, driven, you might have said, from pillar
to post, by a desire for wholeness, if not
perfection, and queried by day, by night, the bare
lambent being, washed ashore.

STEPS TO A HIGH PLACE

Making their descent the Bedouin riders broke
into song. To his foreign ear the sounds
teased out of the desert tints
were fire and ash, and he felt crushed
by the grandeur of the site
when at last they filed into the cool
riverbed gorge. Unnerved by the rockcut tombs
fretted into ghostly temples,

the Englishman moved in the shadow of boulders
hugging the margins of the inner
ground—canvas and easel strapped to his donkey.
Only upon beholding the shine
on the blue lizard's back, scuttling
into a gap, half way up the High Place
of Sacrifice, were his fears quelled. Now he'd
paint as a child of the Idumean night.

MÉTIER

FOR HAROLD SCHIMMEL

Circling back to the same scrap
    of land, year after year, the Levant
sparrow-hawk perched in the crown
    of the pine, a thumbnail sketch
        of feathers behind the puckered
        camouflage of needles and cones—white
            chested, swivelnecked—
        a rapid-fire, rapping sound
goading us out, necks craned, to scan the skies;

or else, think of Tarafa sharply reining
    in his mount, staring at vestiges
        of an abandoned desert campsite,
    indigo tattoos on a scavenging hand:
            these are the fleeting
        signs of endurance, taking us
by surprise, if at all, for we flounder
        in the medium, wherever we turn
            it stares back at us,
            like the hawk's vitreous eye;

even now, in the company of friends,
    children hunting for stones
        in the empty lot,
clambering up the steep incline
    with figs in their hands—this too
        is of the abidingly
    mutable, as dusk wraps its infant arms
        around the city; you and I,
    speaking in the graded light,
        by the saltbushes (silvery orache),
of the flux and permanence

of poetry, which is nothing other than
    "this wandering about
        in sensation, in *aisthesis*,"—
    permanence, which is to say
        recurrence, the warm
        parenthetical glow of gazing
at nothing in particular but what's there
        to see, now and again,
    at the close of day, a cool breeze
announcing the riches-
        to-rags shuffle of seasons.

THE MASK OF LIPARI

D.S.

Freed from the grip of the dead, the exact
    imprint of who you were brought to the light of day:
spectral in a luminous field, the abstract
    terracotta sum of all you could, or *would* say.
Not quite Old Cantankerous, one brow raised
    heavenward, the other knit in a scowl,
but an Englishman in mufti, unfazed,
    keeping the right words from running afoul.
So I beheld you, as I stooped to brush
    the dirt from what just might have been your face;
the strangest of trades, removing grit
    off the rough clay surface, where a blush
appears, though nothing now can take your place,
    not even your double retrieved from the pit.

THE GIFT

You bob up light as a cork
    glistening in the sun by the tumbledown
        pier, your body a torque, a live wire
of joy washed in salt spray, while we
    bend over and rake into a floppy hat
        turquoise slivers of Roman glass, and a Filipino
                          day-laborer
on his day off deftly casts his net
    along the reefs—waist-deep he claps
        and shouts, *Hoa-hoa*, driving his supper
into the mesh; the little, ruined
    bay now yours to call
        "Our hideaway" as the sun descends, hand over fist,
    an invisible cord:—Apollonia,

where the water scoops
    and hollows the stone, and staves off nightfall
        churning under the pier,
and ruffles the sounds of other shores
    as we stoop, vigilant to the slurp and lisp
        of its surf, as though the triple hoot of an owl
was what we heard—the spotted little owl,
    Athene noctua, that bobs and waggles
        and swivels its head 180 degrees, to look us in the eye
before we make to leave, dragging our feet—
    though it's only the sea now
        and its motion, suspended in the mind,
    which turns us into idlers on the shore.

OSTRACON II

Peering at the salient, hands thrust
into your greatcoat. Valleys fanning out

on all sides of the limestone ridge
enveloped in mist. Killing time

watching your breath vaporize. *In,*
out. Barely a slur, barely a burr of sound

barring the faint slurp of boots
slogging an invisible path. In vain

scanning the horizon for the signal-fires
of Lachish. Why aren't the beacons flashing

their green firefly gems in the gloom?
Toeing the line of tohu, the plummet of bohu.

HEMATITE

If he wears a seal of hematite, that man will lose
all he owns

LIBRARY OF TIGLATH-PILESER

His beard raked to the waist, the king
dangles by its neck the diminutive
figure of an ibex, an offering

to the deities: the royal dress of
one such goddess falls open at the loins,
another intercedes, her arms

raised, while a third, a warrior god,
tramples his adversary underfoot
and shakes in his fist a key-ring.

The sealcutter knows his craft well—
how best to limn the divine company
on the cartridge-size cylinder, shaped

bowdrilled, and cut with quartz
sand—he has stooped at the waters
of the Tigris, his vision healed.

CICADA

Song held them
breathless, they took
no thought to
eating, drinking,
grew transparent

                as lies, till
                casting off their
                human form
                they
                were reborn

winged—
their "mirrors,"
so-called, the lone
instrument
of
their song.

READING GILGAMESH

Now remember the taming
  of Enkidu, how the wild game
  bolted into the bush
    after he lay with love
  and was satisfied;
he who'd sport with gazelles
  and quench his thirst in their waterholes
was alone and bound in his thoughts
  to the nameless child of pleasure.

Desire confined to the gazing,
  tender ball. Push on,
    urges the month-by-month
  gardener's manual, as if
the yard were the only vantage ground
  from which to sound
    the setting out and return,
  tacit as the trail
of the field slug turning a leaf
  omnivorous (where the dogrose cleaves
to the cypress).

      Push on in April
with the spading and hoeing
  and consider Enkidu, natural man,
    everyone's second self,
  or pet demoniac,
brainpan teeming with word-stems,
  as though the bold figure of companionship
were carved on the transom of every door.

Nodding to sleep in the noon sun
    that springs the dragonfly
        free from its larva; Shams, Shemesh,
Shamash the Protector.
                              Heed the child
that holds your hand. The right words
    prised out of the mouth of what
strange being? The slender volume
    unclasped slips to the ground.

AFTER NINEVEH

*Which came up in a night, and perished
in a night*

JONAH 4:10

FOR MARIUS KOCIEJOWSKI

I

Sitting under no sweet climbing gourd, you're left
with a scrawl of voices, stone enfleshed,
clawing free from a corridor of low reliefs.
The bevelled iron yields to the mallet's blows
and sprung from its cage, the lioness swags

hindlegs dragging: mute display of pluck
in the throes of pain, where the royal shaft has twice
pierced the spine. Gypsum-chiselled slabs
of wall. We turn and toss in our sleep to such sounds,
as time empties its quiver into the breach.

2

Even so the moment returns when you wake
and feast your eyes on the gazelles,

a troop of them now nuzzle the nearly vacant
pockets of memory you insist

on turning inside out, as if there were
something to show. What could the young

woman be telling her pupils who sit
cross-legged, facing the herd? The delicate

quarry about to break into flight . . .
Ashurbanipal kneels in the pit,

torso and head framed by the pliant bow
while a boy keeps him busy

with a steady supply of arrows. Whoosh,
go the children, mocking the scene,

whoosh, as the baffled creatures fall.

SELF-PORTRAIT IN KHAKI

combat-fatigues: booted and stamped
with fierceness, leaning against
the cracked lid of a sarcophagus, half
buried in debris by the hippodrome.
Tyre, '84. Reading Basho in snatches,
when not in the pillbox
facing the rutted, coastal road.
Mitrailleuse. Rolling the moist syllables,
like pin tumblers, in the mouth.
Rounds of fire beyond the filling
station with the cryptic ECOREVE

hanging by a nail above the pump.

"Vanity boxes abandoned in the sedge.
Rare musical instruments, swaddled
in quilt, splash overboard in the mad
scramble to man the small vessels.
This is why even after a thousand
years, the surf riddles the shoreline
with such a melancholic sound."

OSTRACON III

Squinting at the dozen splayed strokes
of the reed pen dipped in soot and oak-gall,
you puzzle out your own words formed
on the wash surface of the shard, softly fired
and red at the edges. Though hardly poetry
("Who is your servant but a dog"), how curiously
satisfying to the eye, the serried ranks

of letters shaped like grappling hooks.
The rip and suture. Biting your lip like a child
as the nib shuttles its uneasy freight.
Odd to feel so drained from so small a task.
The stray curled at the door doesn't even prick up its ears,
when you rise to stretch your legs.

IN THE MONTH OF TAMMUZ

G.P.

I

I can only guess the gist
of Ibn Gabirol's words
locking the rhyme-bearing verse
into place. For my soul

is dismayed and sorely afraid,
reads Zangwill's version (1923),
lifting the phrase
out of Ezekiel's shipwreck,

though even there the Hebrew
might depict a squall at sea,
or else hair standing-on-end.

—Anyhow, I'm tempted to speak
of the precise arrangement of vowels,
how measure was plainly thought

to keep the poem from spoiling
in the reciter's mouth,

and leave it at that.

All those little notes and queries to yourself
rousing you from Oblomov's sleep.

A flourish of your pen,
and Hebrew enveloped you in a fine cloud

extending reticent tendrils of rain.

Tu Fu dreaming of Li Po
might have been dreaming of you, old friend,

as moonlight drenched your room
"to the roof-beams," and you lingered there

on the terrace, before turning in.

WALID IBN YAZID

Summoned from the desert's Empty Quarter,

Ma'abad, your favorite singer, unwinds
his turban to reveal the Seven Golden Odes
embroidered on its surface.

                              "A piece,"
he whispers in your ear, "of the linen cloth
which hung on the wall of the Ka'aba."
But the precious headgear crumbles to dust
the moment you reach for it,

like the powdery Apple of Sodom. Most
reluctant of Caliphs, poet and marksman,
the white oryx leads you to its lair,
tucked in the white marl hills,
and laves your body with its tongue.
Bon vivant, waylaid in the thickets—

camel-thorn and stinkwood—of the Jordan.

FROM THE SECRET HISTORY

Wishing to see her husband's pain
portrayed in bronze, Domitia
set out to stitch
together Domitian's severed body.
Rome's finest sculptors
were challenged to cast a statue
of the man
in his final agony.
The reconstituted figure
was soon erected near the capitol
and may be seen even today.
(So writes Procopius.)

A curious bit of embroidery.
Hadn't the Senate ordered
all statues of the emperor smashed,
his name effaced? And wasn't
his widow just one more conspirator
in Domitian's murder?
In the end Procopius' gaze
fell on the mundane—
a re-assembled statue whose liquid
molten had long hardened
into the shape of one
who in appearance and cruelty
was not unlike his own
protector, Justinian.

TERAPHIM

These standing female
figurines of unknown provenance,
with pinched nose
and hands crudely
cupping stuck-on

pellets for breasts,
broad hipped, stick
in the throat, and gimlet-eyed—
shaped to preside

over the vanquished,
over the mudbrick
household, snug
as a rib cage.

In all strangeness
they watch over our solitude,
these frangible
low-fired images, unhoused
and rudely mute.

THESE BE THE WORDS

In bold Hebrew letters and small English type.
The stiff pages mottled with mildew,
straining the delicate retinal tissue
where the riddled corpse is a hollow, a reed, a cave,
a sheath, and the elders pace the distance
between the pegged-out body, sprawled
in the field, and the nearest city.
    These be the words and the gloss, the Portion
of the Week in the ragged tome propped
against a pile of books, in two shades of black,
like the plumage of the heavy flying
hooded crow. Neither garroted, nor dumped
lynched nor ditched, the cipher
lies in the open field, plowed for the sowing.
    Read on, in mother tongue and father
tongue, half-and-half, in the coarse mix
and weave, like wool and flax. Everyone's here,
sifting the evidence, poking at the dead
weight, dreaming up the lurid finale,
before joining the column of celebrants
winding into the gorge pricked with shrubs
and rockrose, and the wild pistachio
emitting a faint scent of turpentine.
    Such are the laws, the code, the bloodpact
and solemn rite (the simple gestures
of release) resounding in the rough wadi,
as the whetted blade severs the heifer's neck.

OSTRACON IV

Mornings, the fire banked, puttering about
    the compound, you water the seedlings by the fosse,
       then tidy up inside, while the more

ambitious range the hillsides like foxes.
    Sedentary days, even as life on the outside
       seems more frantic, less explicable.

Only yesterday a mere boy slipped by ruse
    between the lines with a message from the open-eyed one:
       "Beware!" Every man's word his burden;

his joy. Hoisted like a first-born
    on broad shoulders. Write it down—every man's
       word—on the potter's cruse.

SIROCCO

Crushed dates kneaded with goat dung
and bits of sand form a paste

to stop up any hole, time and again;
who plods in the dry fog

and what snaps in the dust storm?
Every man at the door

of his swart goathair tent;
when the song ends

we are like small, migratory quail
that plummet to the ground

exhausted, crying "wet-mi-lips,"
in the shifting wind.

WINTER GHAZALS

The water a muddy palette that won't stick
  to any surface except the thought

we'd never been here before, the scene
  inviting as a game of leapfrog.

Dollops of dream material scooped out
  of the bucket and spread on the table

for the children to play with.
  I'm not complaining, just reaching

back with one hand for the familiar
  chair that's no longer there. Unsure

of our coordinates, we round the bend—the finest
  secrets: dust between uncut pages.

*

Then why not admit the bright light
  shimmering on the horizon isn't the windfall

we'd been half expecting, your "Any day now,"
  closing in on us. One more metaphor

wriggling its ears. It's like riding in the open
  cockpit of a crop duster,

keeping tabs on your every move. Sometimes, water
  lapping at my feet, I replay in my mind

the oddest scenes and bits of dialogue.
  Open any book, at any page, and you'll uncover

something of our lives. Blue's the color to ward off
  the jinn who won't be reminded of heaven.

SCRIPT

Who spoke, man or woman?
Some said the former, others shook their heads
"Surely this is the voice of a woman,"
while yet a third suggested
not one but three voices at play. I copied down
on a scrap of paper lines translated
from the chalk wall of Apollophanes' tomb,
beginning:
                    "There's nothing that I can do
for you, no way to please you, I sleep with someone else,"
and thought no more of the matter,
until months later, ferried back from Athos
        (where the brazen and quick
        and the lean stragglers—shuffling at the end
        of the line—stepped down the ramp)
I rummaged in my satchel,
while lounging on the beach in Ouranoupoli,
and retrieved the message
hastily penciled in the white chamber.

An hour's drive from home,
we'd cautiously made our way
into the bell-shaped pits,
the musicians' tomb, and the vast,
underground pigeon-house.
                    "But it is you I love,
dearest," so *she* speaks, "by Aphrodite,
I'm glad about one thing,
you've left me your coat as a pledge."
And then came the line
which left us short of breath

when we first discovered the inscription
within the Sidonian cave:
                    "But I flee, and permit you expanses
of freedom."
                    Is this the voice of the deceased?
"Do anything you like,
but don't strike the wall, it makes such noise,
we'll motion to each other,
that will be the sign between us."

I dug my heels in the warm sand,
unable to disentangle in my mind the sound
of the hickory staff on the stone paths
of the Holy Mountain, with that of the distant,
baffling voice.
                    A young woman slumbered
on her side in the treacherous sun,
her hair swept up, exposing the nape of her neck.
Arms covering her breasts in a V.
Her companion narrowed his eyes at the goldleaf
dusting the Aegean.
                    How beautiful she was.
Theophanes of Crete, might have painted her—
with a brush made from an ass's mane—
as the Theotokos, mother of God,
in burnt umber and terra verte,
applying light tones for the flesh,
and for the pupil
"black gathered from the smoke of pinewood."

IN ALEXANDRIA

AFTER YEHUDA HALEVI

Has time taken off its clothes of trembling
and decked itself out in riches,
and has the earth put on fine-spun linen
and set its beds in gold brocade?
All the fields of the Nile are checkered,
as though the bloom of Goshen
were woven straps of a breastplate,
and lush oases dark-hued yarn,
and Raamses and Pithom laminated goldleaf.
    Girls on the riverbank, a bevy of fawns,
linger, their wrists heavy with bangles—
anklets clipping their gait.
                        The heart enticed
forgets its age, remembers boys or girls
in the garden of Eden, in Egypt, along the Pishon,
running on the green to the river's edge;
the wheat is emerald tinged with red,
and robed in needlework;
it sways to the whim of the sea breeze,
as though bowing in thanks to the Lord . . .

SANCTUARY

Paphos

A burst of molten rock erupts
    from the floor
        of the Middle
  Sea. Sly-eyed

laughter-loving goddess:
    lisp of ripple marks
        along the sun
  riffed margin, where a goatpath

clambers up the crescent
    bay. Far above,
        bare summits, stripped
  of their riches, but

for the roadside flora,
    umbel and asphodel,
        stoking the syllables
  banked within—

Larnaca

The rose
pleats of the loin-
cloth remain,
the rest has long been peeled

away from the wood
where John and Mary,
and the angel—
still bearing their tinctures—

look askance from the poles
of the cross,
lost, it seems,
in the mind's rigging.

DJERBA

He pressed as he spoke
a black cylinder to his throat
galvanizing the punctured

remains of his voicebox:

*C'est la nuit de 'Id
el-Kabir.*

        Lean knife-sharpeners
set up shop on the streets—

    push-pedal whetstones

spinning. Island of the Lotus
Eaters.

        Rank sheepskins
are stacked by the kiosk

and pitched into the dawn
van, idling.

OSTRACON V

Cedarwood and rushes, oleander and flax tow
    bound, kindled and flashed like a flare
        from a city built on its mound
of rubble. The last bootless
        display of hope siphoned heavenward;
then the quick erosion and collapse, and the song
    plucked out of the muddle. Even now
        the figures file off through the gate
tower into the perilous landscape,
        tuning their lyres for the long march.

Another message, perhaps the last, dispatched
    from the post perched on the spur.
        Hastily penned in a flowing hand, the ink
running on occasion into hairline
        fractures in the surface of the pottery.
The final word in the packet—your little dossier—
    destined to end up in whose hands?
        This evening, when Tobshillim
    arrives, I shall send your letter up
        to the city . . . That very moment

EGERIA'S TRAVELS

You who trudged into the arid interior,
and out again, unruffled, though certainly humbled,
like the dew-soaked lily. *Remember me*
echoes in the dry torrent beds
where tumbleweed once raised brittle fists
and the sandstorm obliterated the space
around you who put down for your reverend sisters
in the west "in plain words,"
all that the keen eye sees. Your journal, lost,
then found centuries later,
bound in someone else's tract (*On the Mysteries*)
is today's potion for the unhouseled mind.
Hymns and antiphons, Gethsemane at cock-crow.
An itinerary crammed with miraculous
place-names. But now the rockdove's
bruised, summer notes ricochet in the courtyard
where the heat rivets the city to its rack.

THE FEAST OF THE GODS

They could be a loose band of rustics
    on their day off, unencumbered, free to fiddle away

their time as much as they please.
    I can just see clutched in Apollo's hands

the lira da braccio poking up behind
    a young god's sturdy thighs, who is lifting the hem

of Lotis-the-maiden's slip. (She sleeps
    unsuspecting to the end.)
                    And isn't that old Silenus,

draped in orange and attending
    to his proverbial ass, whose strenuous *he-haw*

will bring these dubious gods to their feet?

The painted figures slip in and out of mind,
    like "outdoor," acid overtones

in a wind ensemble, that refuse to inscribe
    themselves in anyone's roster.
                    To translate, with a sound

and certain eye, the temperament
    of these distant relations

into the poise and fluency of form, had been his hidden,
    pressing agenda, propped

in front of the canvas—even as his heart gave.

ROMANESQUE

He might have been trained in the workshops
of southern Italy before boarding ship
for the Latin Kingdom. The hand
that chiselled the irregular line
highlighting dejection, then joy's lips
on each side of the holy-water basin in Acre
could have carved also,
according to Barasch, the angel-heads
of Monopoli;—the resemblances
are striking: the same low forehead
and broad nose, the same oversized, bulging eyes
and slight asymmetry of the mouth;
the same distribution, in short,
of bulk, and indifference to pictorial
or graphic effects. The anonymous
artist undoubtedly delighted in the sheer
act of modeling; though speaking
of opposing moods of sadness
and joy, Barasch touches suggestively
on intentions beyond mere craft,
so that even now circling the vessel
in the vaulted room, we too
might wipe away tears from every face
and smiling broadly emerge, alive
to new meaning in plain sentiment.

IN THE MANNER OF PETRARCH

FOR ELI LEVIN

Hunched down on your knees over the face
on the bar-room floor. Who is it the brush
consigns to your care? The features a touch
childlike: slit eyes, ding-dong nose, a gothic taste
for the telling line; the same downsweep
of the mouth, in fact, as in Martini's art,
though drifters pressing round you and a tart-
faced barfly usurp the latter's upsweep
of angels and saints. Carry on, if only to nail
love vainly to the boards. She of the blank
cadences and gentle eyes will not fail
to elude your grasp. Might this be the thank-
less lesson, softly announcing its toll?—
"where the flesh casts a shadow on the soul."

THE HEAVENLY LADDER

But I have not yet been able to leave myself behind
ST BASIL

Olive, hickory, oak, or the pliable maple, whittle your staff
and become as sounding brass

as you follow the winding mule trail,
but keep in mind Maximus, who'd torch his shack to ashes

and further up scree and boulder scale at the sound
of newcomers approaching—

a burnt hut for each rung of the heavenly ladder
with no shelter, or anywhere to flee.

A turquoise armored beetle whizzes by your cheek,
its low buzz pitching you off balance.

Sit under the wild plum tree and embrace
your friend penury, nurse of philosophy,

where time has blanched the face in the triangle
above the portal, for poverty kindles

the tapering cypress, and the wall that crumbles
at your touch, into a brightness

of the mind.—Not the Abbot's "inexplicable joy,"
in seeing the miraculous, Tabor light

turn the ribcage into a Chinese lantern
(eyes shut, chin against chest, in the room's darkest corner)

but a dram of dusk light clutched in the talons
of the peregrine, wheeling slowly over the hermits' valley

as toads in the brush pitch, into the mesh of leaves,
the low, ruined chords of their hallelujahs.

RUMI IN THE HAMMAM

Soft-bellied Mevlana swathed in a towel-wrap
shuffles into the hot baths. He runs his coarse
mitten over my body, and the painted figures
awake from sooty sleep, open their eyes
wide as jonquils. He scours my chest hard
and fast, and the Seljuk maidens in goldleaf
pantaloons cup hands to their ears,
as though catching the strains of *oud* and reed
in the air. Mevlana bends my legs back
over my head like the poplars of Anatolia
flexed for warping, and from the domed
ceiling Tabrizi breaks into his antelope grin.
Mevlana plunges a bowl into the hot-and-cold
basin, and douses me with water. Men sit up
dazed on the marble slab, for a moment
slipping into boyhood; the sleek
wall-figures step out of their onion skins;
and there's Hodja the prankster, riding
his donkey backward and crowing like a rooster.
The amazing keeper of the baths digs
his fingers into my scalp and swivels my head
in its socket till the dust of Konya rises
and settles in the grasslands. He breathes
sharply like a winded horse, but his work
isn't done, *doubt* must be sweated out
of every pore. Why isn't that poor Yunus
rolling on the floor like a polo ball?
I swat feebly at the airy column of steam.
"Jonas, is that you, so recently spat
onto these shores?" And before getting an answer
Mevlana covers me in soap suds for a last

gentle rub down. Rising to my feet soft
as lokum, I'm shepherded into the warm room
and all the hovering figures sink back
into the flystrip-yellow walls. *Güle Güle*
the bathkeeper calls out, "Go smiling,"
his voice booms all moonshine behind me.

IN PAMUKKALE

I'd been walking in circles in the hooded
dark of the village below Hierapolis' white ridge,
   trying to relocate the whereabouts

of my pension, when I first heard
the high whiplash, followed by a wilful throb,
   a sort of deadpan guffaw, the doubled

voice of a ventriloquist, pitched
across the empty lot. Ah, I said, and loitered,
   intent upon threading
the needle of its song. And the mountains

on all sides huddled solemn as Hittites
lying in wait in the high passes. Ah, I repeated,
   as I turned down the road, what
signs and wonders lead me on.

AS THE WINDS VEER

in periplum

Curious to find even here the round-
leafed henbit, on the road to Asklepieion,
sun tingling pate scorched as the tough
hillside bramble only goats stomach.
    I imagine running into so-and-so, "Hatless
my boy, in this heat?" and reach back
for slouch hat in hip pocket, slap
its soft brim against my thigh, and the dust
of travel billows and fades: Port Said,
Limassol, Rhodes, then the slow ferry
to Cos lying, sea-girt, like a spitted sheep;
and, later, the Lydian coastline,
half a day's unruffled sailing to the east.
    Did the herdsmen's words fly
like the roadside pebbles that sang off
your shoes, Theocritus? Tramping up
Mt Dikeos, just below Zia,
tucked in the rockface cleft,
I stop for a breather, and, taking
in the view, can't help but see
in the looming coast the figure of my own child
nimbly stepping out of a coldwater
pool, flushed as wild celery. Smile
at the travel-induced correspondence,
like overwrought dreams in unfamiliar lodgings.
First night on the island,
I jot down such a strange specimen—

Who's this with contorted brows
following the sign of the perforated heart
    carved on the sidewalk? So many
faces stream by: heavy-lidded
    and snub-nosed, thick-lipped
and hollow-cheeked, and here's one
    with hair combed into the shape
of an amphora.
                  —Dear Ephesians,
    won't you recognize one of your own
cradling Arcadia out of the cave
    of the Seven Sleepers? Knobbly
kneed, soaking up the first rays
    of the sawtoothed sun, sans theorem
to square the day, hillflanks
    hemorrhaging poppies, and shoreward
the long quays long sunk in silt.
    —*Lord, protect us in our sleep,*
save us when we wake, inscribed over
    the gateway. Even now, somewhere
between Cape Rough and the Crumbles,
    the cows low in the meadows,
like brokers sobbing into their pillows.

The crosslegged Old Kingdom granite scribe
doesn't bat an eye as we brush shoulders,
so I leave him there, clutching a stylus
for dear life. Drowsy port town, a crush
of cranes and twin minarets, like sparring
partners, poke at the ether's soft belly;
paying out their lines under a plinth,
a band of tiros point at the absent statue
and exclaim, "Lesseps"—who dealt the first blow

that pierced the isthmus: the long
jump east. Voices, as the winds veer.
  "At night, when the fatal hour seemed
to approach, I spoke at length with two friends,
at a club-house table, on painting and
music, defining from my point of view
the origin of colors and the meaning
of numbers. One of them, named Paul,
wanted to accompany me, but I told him
I wasn't going home. 'Where are you
off to?' he asked. *Toward the Orient!*"

  "Ships upon ships. A perpetual
coming and going between the sea
    and the interior." The poet from Smyrna
returns to the boarded-up home
    of his childhood; returns
like the endangered monk seal
    to the hideaway cove of his boyhood.
  —Voices from the bottleneck
ports, garbled in the wind,
    blurred and pumiced in the spindrift
like the Marine Venus dredged up
    from the old harbor in Rhodes
(Mandraki—The Sheepfold—lying
    in the shadow of the swallow-tailed
battlements). The sea unrolls
    its granular voiceprint on the shore,
and the poet from Smyrna watches
    four men struggle to lower by rope
a worn-out commode from a back-
    street balcony. Here is decay,
he writes, without resurrection.

—Ships upon ships. One city
is torched, another raises its phalloi
    in the cinders. But look hard
in the light of the everlasting fire
    that flares and dies, and you can
trace the Greek letters on the quayside
    as stevedores unload the holds
in a perpetual coming and going.

Approaching with her familiar
easy smile and good looks, her figure bifurcated
like a river rounding an outcrop of rock
into two identical bodies, so that at first
I thought I was seeing double and vigorously shook
my head. Nothing changed, each separate self
strode forward, as though wading through
a spring meadow. I couldn't take my eyes off
the two, and gasped again as one of the figures
proved diaphanous, melting into whatever
stood in the way. So this is the soul,
I told myself, catching my breath
—wise and dry as a beam of light.
    So she spoke, pressing upon me softly
the full contents of her dream, like a salve
to soothe the heart. Stirred by the new
intelligence, I was a one-eyed
Polyphemus gazing at the brine that frothed
the shore—he who'd never win Galatea
of the sea. Go on, stare at the blue sheen,
bark all you want at this complex
of islets, of peninsulas and deep mountainfolds
(sheep flecking the spur like felspar)
where Galatea's still entangled like thistledown
in the eye's mesh of rods and cones.

Pear-shaped, with long neck and toe
base offering a firm grip, these amphoras
    heaped on seabed are all that's left of ship
that neither squall nor shoal brought down
    but the dreaded mollusc boring into its timbers
(wood rasped to a fine dust by micro-
        scopic teeth). These large, two-handled jugs
languish beyond reach like odalisques
    that make our senses swim. Stamped
with the lily of Rhodes, here's one destined
    to quench whose thirst? Aristaeus, Memnon,
Nicias: Names impressed in soft clay,
    then fired in the kiln, ring distant-
familiar—for the quick soul's
    exhaled from moist things.
—Swimming shoreward, I leisurely scan
the near-empty beach where bladderwrack
is raked into low mounds and a scruffy mutt
runs circles round a woman in mauve latex.
No one has bothered to untangle the tight-
lipped deckchairs stacked near the kiosk. Stroke
upon stroke, till feet graze bottom. How keep
last night's dream intact? The beguiling
amphoras. It was Nicias—no?—who wrote back
to his friend these lines: "What you say
is right, Theocritus. Eros has made poets
of many who never wrote a line before . . ."

BREATH IN THE FRIEZE

Pech Merle

Breath, you said, in the frieze where mammoth buck,
in the warm afflatus of the hollow femur—
manganese oxide mixed in urine, or fat
from the marrow—the hands exhaled
above the dappled horses, back to cursive
back, overlaying the tapering fish;

and again, you drew breath from creatures
in polychrome, deep in the sanctum's warren
of chambers, and from small incisions
that conjured woman in the folds of the wall—
the familial spirits and rank bestiary,
caught in the laser-pen's minim of light;

even by the limestone weir, you breathed in
where mother and child trod, and left their prints—
oak root boring down into the gallery
in search of moisture—lungs inhaling their poppy
of air among the whiplash contours
and spell of the doubly wise, as they step

out of their skins, into the mirror kingdom.

Notes

Imago   The dragonfly, "attuned to life on the wing," goes through ten to fifteen molts before its nymphal skin splits and it achieves full adulthood.

Ostracon Poems   The staggered sequence is indebted to H. Torczyner's commentary and translations from the palaeo-Hebrew of eighteen inscribed potsherds, or ostraca (dating from the sixth century BC). Known as the Lachish Letters, the shards were uncovered among the debris of a ruined guardroom during the 1932–38 excavations of the ancient fortified city of Lachish.

Steps to a High Place   In 1924 the British painter David Bomberg and his wife Alice left their temporary residence in Jerusalem, and spent six months in the barely accessible "rose-red city" of Petra in Transjordan, located on the ancient spice route of the east. Camping out in a large marquee, on loan from the Emir Abdulla, and under the watchful eye of ten Bedouin escorts, Bomberg set out to paint the strangeness of the Nabatean city of sandstone tombs, temples, and mountain-top sacrificial altars.

Métier   Tarafa Ibn al-Abd was a member of the noble tribe of Bakr, which roamed about the Persian Gulf. He is considered one of the great pre-Islamic poets, who extolled in their *qasidas* the austerities and pleasures of desert life. Legend has it that his ode was one of the seven "suspended" poems, or *Mu'allaqat,* transcribed in letters of gold on fine Egyptian linen and suspended from the Ka'aba in Mecca.

Walid Ibn Yazid   Walid Ibn Yazid briefly held the title of the Umayyad Caliph in 743 AD. The British archeologist R.W. Hamilton has suggested that the elaborately constructed palace and pleasure dome of Khirbet Al Mafjar near Jericho was built by the rakish poet, and not by his rather austere uncle, the Caliph Hisham.

The Mask of Lipari　The citizens of the Greek colony of Lipari in the third century BC were such avid fans of the new comedy, exemplified by the plays of Menander, that they chose to take with them to the next world the mask of their favorite character. During excavations in the 1960s and 1970s the archeologist Luigi Bernabo Brea uncovered a complete repertory of such terracotta masks buried in the island's necropolis.

Self-Portrait in Khaki　The last stanza adapts lines from the English version (translated by Nobuyuki Yuasa) of Basho's "Records of a Travel-worn Satchel."

These Be the Words　Cf. Deuteronomy 21: 1–10.

Script　The four-line tomb inscription was found in ancient Mareshah, some forty kilometers west of Jerusalem, where the Ptolemies established a Sidonian colony in the third century BC. Theophanes of Crete established himself as a painter of frescoes on Mount Athos in the sixteenth century. Two centuries later Dionysios of Fourna, also a resident of Athos, described in great detail the materials and techniques, as well as the hagiography, of painting frescoes in *The Painter's Manual.*

In Alexandria　Born in northern Spain some time before 1075, Yehuda Halevi was the preeminent Hebrew poet of twelfth-century Andalusia and author of the religious treatise *The Book of the Kuzari*. In 1140, hoping to reach the Holy Land, he sailed for Alexandria, where he tarried for close to a year. The poem—written as the opening of a letter to a friend in Cairo—seems to suggest that the land of Goshen reawakened in the old poet youthful desires, which he struggled to align with his profoundly religious sensibility. Halevi did finally embark for the Syro-Palestinian coast in September 1141, though when and how he died remains a mystery.

Egeria's Travels　Egeria, a Christian pilgrim, journeyed to the Middle East between 381 and 384 AD. Her Latin journals were lost for some seven hundred years. About a third of her text, however, resurfaced in Italy in the late nineteenth century. I make use of the 1972 English translation by John Wilkinson.

The Feast of the Gods Signed and dated by Giovanni Bellini in 1514, the painting was never completed because of the painter's advanced age. In the end Titian was summoned, and he may have repainted parts of the landscape.

The Heavenly Ladder In the early sixteenth century a certain Greek Orthodox monk living on Mount Athos claimed that after a long period of fasting and meditation on his navel, he could see the divine light of Mount Tabor. A hermit's movement of enthusiasts rapidly developed on the narrow peninsula stretching into the Aegean sea. Opposition was voiced against the "navel-souled-ones" and in true Byzantine fashion a heated, prolonged dispute ensued between the two camps. A manuscript still exists by Abbot Xerocarca describing the spiritual rigors required as a preliminary to beholding the uncreated light.

Rumi in the Hammam The figure of Mevlana Rumi as keeper of the hot baths leans on A.J. Arberry's version of lyric 101 in his *Mystical Poems of Rumi* (University of Chicago Press, 1968).

As the Winds Veer "Cape Rough" and the "Crumbles" are mentioned in a verse fragment by Hipponax, a native of Ephesus who lived in the sixth century BC. The lines beginning "At night, when the fatal hour . . ." are translated from Gérard de Nerval's *Aurelia*. The fourth section crystallizes around George Seferis's journal entries from July to October, 1950.

Some Recent Poetry from Anvil

Heather Buck
Waiting for the Ferry

Nina Cassian
Take My Word for It

Peter Dale
Edge to Edge
SELECTED POEMS

Dick Davis
Touchwood

Carol Ann Duffy
The Pamphlet
The World's Wife
LIMITED EDITION
Time's Tidings (ed.)
GREETING THE 21ST CENTURY

Martina Evans
All Alcoholics Are Charmers

Michael Hamburger
Collected Poems 1941–1994
Late

Donald Justice
Orpheus Hesitated Beside the Black River
NEW AND SELECTED POEMS 1952–1997

Marius Kociejowski
Music's Bride

Peter Levi
Reed Music

Thomas McCarthy
Mr Dineen's Careful Parade
NEW AND SELECTED POEMS

Stanley Moss
Asleep in the Garden
NEW AND SELECTED POEMS

Dennis O'Driscoll
Weather Permitting
POETRY BOOK SOCIETY RECOMMENDATION

Sally Purcell
Fossil Unicorn

Peter Russell
The Elegies of Quintilius

Peter Scupham
Night Watch

Ruth Silcock
A Wonderful View of the Sea

Daniel Weissbort
What Was All the Fuss About?